An Italian Honeymoon

Eric Wilhite

DEDICATION

For Jennie, obvi.

CONTENTS

1: TO MILAN

On planes, being tall sucks. Simple truth. Somewhere over the Atlantic my knees begin that dull ache able to drive the most Zen of characters to insanity. Jennie is curled up into a little ball against the window looking content, if not comfortable.

We began in Knoxville, TN. Our plane to Chicago O'Hare was delayed and eventually cancelled due to maintenance issues. Luckily, we were quick to the counter to get a change. Neither of us were too keen to hop on a plane with four hours' worth of maintenance problems. After hearing our honeymoon plans, the attendant graciously flipped us to another airline. We left immediately, connected in Atlanta, and with a short turnaround were in the air for Milan. Unfortunately in all of the changing we lost our premium seat upgrade. Bye bye, extra 4 inches of legroom.

We were due to arrive in Milan at 8:30am. I tried my best to sleep. I even slipped on the provided sleep mask and feigned a light snore. But I couldn't come up with more than 20 minutes of broken napping at a time. Jennie was slightly more successful. But both of us spent the majority of our 8 1/2 hour flight drooling in a daze at the headrest entertainment system.

Around 7:00am Italian time, the flight tracker showed us flying over Europe. Excitement began to really grip us. Before long, a group of ladies was gathering around an open window. They were pointing and gawking at something below. Amateurs, I thought. But then, Jennie slid up her window. Light poured through. Once our eyes adjusted, The Alps spread out below us and into the horizon. The snow-capped tips cut into the sky with a sharpness foreign to my Smoky Mountains frame of reference. I couldn't imagine a better kickoff to our journey.

Touchdown. Standing up feels great. Blood flow slowly returns to my legs, but I can already feel the fatigue of broken sleep. It's a long walk from the terminal to customs. Once there, the agent appears to have gotten about as much sleep as we did. He barely gives us a glance as he stamps and points us through.

In the main lobby, people are waiting with signs and balloons and streamers. We try to joke about how it's nice Italy would throw us a welcoming party, but our droopy eyes can barely squint to smile.

We follow the arrows directing us to a shuttle train. My card doesn't work in the self-serve ticket machine. No problem, we brought a different card connected to another account. But after 2 desperate swipes, it doesn't work either. After a brief moment of despair, an employee circles around and directs us through a door and to a counter. The woman behind the counter speaks better English than me (Jennie will tell you this is not much of an accomplishment thanks to an East Tennessee twang.) Our cards work fine on her machine, and we scurry downstairs to make the train.

Once you get your train ticket, you have to validate it before you can get on. There are small, green boxes affixed around the platform at all Italian stations. Sometimes they are visible. More often than not, they are nowhere to be seen. A rookie traveler in Italy could very easily overlook these. But if you are caught by an attendant on the train with a non-validated ticket you'll face a hefty fine. Luckily, in my OCD-level research of our trip, I had come across this. So we watched as a sharply dressed Italian family marched up to the puncher machine and validated the tickets and quickly followed suit.

From Malpensa airport it is about an hour's ride to Milano Centrale. Large, concrete apartment complexes rise up on the outskirts of the city. We sit facing each other, in a daze. The train stops a few times, and mostly teenagers with questionable haircuts and hygiene get on. I don't understand the fashion in my own country, so I try not to judge. But a shaved side mullet? If you insist, Giacomo.

We pass through the industrial sector and into the city proper. Our hotel isn't far from the station and just before we pull into the covered terminal I can see the back side of it.

After months of anticipation, we are here at last.

An Italian Honeymoon.

2: MILAN

Rows upon rows of train lines all spill out together into Milano Centrale. People run every which way, most with a mixture of frenzy and desperation on their faces. The loudspeaker is calling out departures, platform changes, cancellations. I quickly become claustrophobic and we make haste for the exit.

The lobby of Milano Centrale is no relief. A series of switchback escalators and shops will leave even the most seasoned train hopper aghast. We search for the ticket machine to secure our spot to Corniglia, the smallest seaside town in the Cinque Terre the next morning. Again our cards fail. The line at the service desk winds out the glass doors and around the corner. So we set out to find an ATM, and use the cash only self-serve machines.

We are grumpy. And hot. Like throat crushing can't breathe hot. We have landed in Italy amidst an unusual heatwave, with temperatures hovering somewhere between devil's armpit and surface of a thousand suns. So when the two ATM's in the terminal are out of order, (no doubt to drive tourists to the high-fee "Change" shops) we give up. We make for the exit, praying for any kind of breeze.

Out the main doors, we rejoice in our first breath of (semi) fresh air since Knoxville. With the air, we are greeted to Italy by the usual tourist preying immigrant street salesmen. As we drag through coos and demonstrations, Jennie and I both are surprised by their offerings.

We have both done our fair share of travel. As such, we are used to the souvenirs and cheaply made trinkets. Carved Mayan blocks and panther calls in Mexico. Soccer unis and flamenco CD's in Spain. But here, in perhaps the most poignant and revealing sign of our digital reliance, they are hawking selfie-sticks and USB power banks. No thanks. We've packed our own.

Our stiff and sleepless bodies whine with every step. We're just a minute into walking before I am thanking the backpack gods that we packed light. I had studied the maps for hours back home, and knew the routes to and fro. We are over one block, and up a couple from the station.

Hotel Terminal is a low key place. Simply adorned, with a small lobby. The main selling point is its proximity to the station. Especially now that we are exhausted. We arrive around 11:00am, but the receptionist crushes our dreams of a nap. He tells us to come back in an hour or so. We drop off our bags with him and wander back into the street.

Figuring our cards won't work most places, we stock up on cash at an ATM. The heat gives us an excuse to duck into a tiny cafe for our first taste of famed Italian espresso. It's a narrow place, and there's just a few locals inside. One at the bar, two at a table in the back. The woman behind the bar greets us with a smile. I muster up an elementary hello, and she lists off the options. Jennie, the coffee connoisseur, orders a traditional shot. I, the coffee noob, go for an Americano.

I had never tasted coffee before Jennie came along. But when you aim to marry a woman who has worked exclusively in the coffee business, you pick up the taste for it fairly quickly. In the 8 months and 3 days between our first date and our marriage, I soaked up all kinds of coffee knowledge. Now, I am quite the coffee snob myself.

Still, I defer to her assessment on quality. And she claims her first taste of Italian espresso was very good. My Americano was served so piping hot I had to wait 20 minutes just to sip it. And even then my torched tongue couldn't taste a thing. But on a positive note, the AC was directly above us. We drooped in our chairs and passed the time observing our surroundings.

The woman behind the bar speaks no English, but when she came around and cleaned off our table she fires off some rapid Italian and points toward the bar. We figure the exchange amounts to: "Thank you for your business but please leave, you cold air moochers." So we pay and walk up a block to a convenience store. We search for cold drinks, but none are to be found. A little ways more and there is a vending machine cubby hole tucked into the building. We get a couple of waters, but neither are cold. Bummer.

Back at the hotel our room is ready. We grab our bags and head up the stairs. It's a nice space. A good size bed, flanked by outlets and tables, and a recently updated bathroom. The AC has been turned off, so the dead air in the room is toasty. We switch it on, and I take an icy cold shower to cool off. By the time I'm out, Jennie is snoring. The wall unit is still blowing lukewarm so I fiddle with the switches. After a few minutes I give up, and give in to the heatwave. I plop down and pass out.

Hot as it was, I'm not sure a more satisfying or restorative nap has ever been taken. We wake up around 5:00pm, and stretch and clean ourselves up. Milan is well known for its high fashion, so we are likely going to appear out of place regardless of our hygiene or choice of garment.

Outside, the mid-day sun has mercifully eased, but the

heat still radiates off the streets. We retrace our steps back to Milano Centrale, and after successfully using the cash-only machine for our tickets to Corniglia the next morning, we head down the stairs near the building's imposing front columns. The Metro line will drop us off in the main square of the city, just in front of the Duomo di Milano. But, in our next futile attempt at self-service, our bills are too big for the Metro machine. A guy comes over and offers us a smaller bill. At first, I take his offer thinking he is perhaps an employee there to make change, but I realize he isn't uniformed in any kind of way. He instructs me to use his money in the machine and something feels off. I hand him back his money, grab Jennie's hand, and walk off. We both agree that something was amiss about the interaction. We turn back to look, and the guy had already moved on to another foreign traveler, making the same offer, and giving the same instructions. Maybe he's just a Good Samaritan. But I have my doubts.

We approach an attendant window at the bottom of the steps. In my best Italian, I order us 4 local tickets, 2 going, and 2 coming back. The attendant seems pleased with my feeble attempt at her language, and quickly exchanges the money for the tickets. We breeze past the turnstiles, the Good Samaritan still lurking near the machines, and down onto the platform. The train arrives quickly and we zip off towards downtown.

Walking up out of the Metro, we emerge quite literally in the main square. I can't ride a Metro without remarking about how they should be cherished civic achievements. Miles and miles of tunnels bored directly beneath enormous cities for the sake of quick and easy travel. If we ever move to a large city, I'll gladly trade in my car for a Metro card.

Late afternoon makes for a nice time to stroll Milan's streets. Most of the tourists are tuckered out, and you are left with their few holdouts and the meandering locals.

Standing in the Piazza del Duomo, we spin and try to get our bearings. The cathedral rises up before us. It took nearly 600 years to complete, and it's easy to see why. The striking Gothic architecture and intricate details make it hard for your eyes to settle in one place. Spires point to the heavens, while sculpture pieces adorn every nook and cranny. It's huge, the 5th largest church in the world, and in Italy it is only eclipsed by St. Peters. I think it is best described by Mark Twain in his *Innocents Abroad* as "so vast... and yet so delicate."

The piazza is surrounded by shops and restaurants. Turning from the cathedral, we spot a small gelato place. We turn to each other in excitement and make directly for it. There are loads of choices, and everything sounds so darn good. It's unfair that they make you choose. If my depth of Italian vocabulary wasn't so shallow, I would have asked for a sampler buffet. In the end, Jennie and I share the same brain and settle on vanilla and Nutella. Ice cream is generally a bit heavy on my tummy. But this gelato, mmm. I always had room for more.

Cones in hand, we mosey past some shops through a covered galleria, and up the Via Dante. Milan was planned as more of a rest and recovery point for us, so we just walked without a plan. The city itself has a much older personality than I was expecting. Of late, Milan has been hailed as the progressive, forward thinking city of Italy. With modern fashion, financial centers, and sleek new buildings. But the area we were now exploring retains a charm from an earlier time. The old concrete and plaster buildings are decorated with gorgeous trim, details often (sadly) lacking in modern architecture.

Following Via Dante, just past one of those quintessentially European leader on a horse monuments, we come to a large fountain back dropped by an impressive castle. Locals sit on the edge of the fountain dipping their feet in to cool off. So, when in Milan, do as the Milanese do. We slip off our shoes and dip our feet in the water.

Young kids play in the water. They run through the arcing streams splashing each other, and occasionally, the feet soaking onlookers. Selfie-stick guys circle the fountain, repeatedly poking them in people's faces and getting shut down. They are so commonplace in Italy that soon they fade into the background. A minor annoyance in an otherwise beautiful country.

A quick drip dry and we decide to check out the fortress in front of us. Castello Sforzesco, the Sforza Castle, was built by the Duke of Milan in the 15th century. It is a large and unexpected break from the downtown cityscape. The main gate was once only accessible by drawbridge over a moat. My imagination instantly fills the medieval moat with alligators and other scary people eaters, but sadly it was just a ditch with water. Today, the water is gone and a permanent bridge crosses over the remaining ditch.

The courtyard is pretty and well-manicured. The Castle interior closed just before we made it in, and there are a few frescoes by Leonardo da Vinci I would have liked to have seen. But we'll most certainly get our fill of art on this trip, so my disappointment is muffled. A sparsely attended concert for the ongoing Expo Milan is happening on the right side of the courtyard. An overly enthusiastic announcer introduces a jam band, and they proceed to perform for about 10 people. We feel a bit bad for the band, but not bad enough to make their crowd 12. So we make our rounds of the courtyard and I sneak a few pictures of Jennie as she twirls and makes goofy faces.

It hits me again just how crazy I am for her. Rewind 10 months, and a poll of my friends and family would have been nearly unanimous. Nobody, including myself, thought I was the settle down type. I had a couple of girlfriends growing up, but my focus was always on other things. I was (am) into nerdy stuff, and sports, and travel, and never made relationships a priority.

Jennifer turned all of that upside down. Or more accurately, right side up. Our first date was a hike on the Tennessee-North Carolina line that normally takes about 2 hours. We stopped at every single overlook and talked for hours. About everything. Life, our past, our future, our likes and dislikes. Heck, we even talked about our spirit animals. A 2 hour hike turned into a 6 hour conversational stroll.

From that day on, we were nearly inseparable. We fell in love so quickly that everyone around us had raised eyebrows. Those closest to us could sense the change though. My family especially. My mom wagered it would be 6 months before Jennie joined the family. Close. 4 months after our first date we were engaged. 4 more, and we had a simple ceremony under a tree in the Smoky Mountains.

So as we walked the courtyard I couldn't help but reflect on our whirlwind of a love story. No couple's relationship is perfect, but we work really hard to meet each other's needs for love and support. Jennie is the smart, incredibly kind, beautiful, sometimes hard-headed, and always loving woman of my dreams.

Returning from my mushy thoughts and googly eyes, we exit medieval Milan and return to the present. Crossing the bridge, our stomachs begin to cry out. We haven't eaten much of substance since our airplane breakfast, so we set out in search of supper. We pass a few tourist trap restaurants, recognizable worldwide by their attractive hosts stalking you down the sidewalk waving menus in English. No thanks.

We agree our best bet is to break off down an alley. So we do, zig-zagging away from the wide avenues and into small, cobblestone streets. After a few minutes, we happen upon an old stony building with a restaurant called Andry discretely welcoming guests. We walk in, finding it small but charming. We are seated immediately. The waiter (thankfully) speaks a word or two of English, but our fellow patrons seem to all be local. Passionate Italian conversations are held all around us. Wine bottles line the walls and green vines hang from the upper level.

I go for a creamy scallop pasta, and Jennie chooses a pizza. We order a bottle of water and some wine. By this point we are starving, and when the food arrives we make short work of it. On top of our hunger, we hadn't noticed just how dehydrated we had gotten. With wine being almost mandatory in the Italian dining experience, we wonder if we will turn out unintentionally tipsy for most of the trip.

We let out our belts a bit and pay. Night has fallen and Jennie tells me that it has cooled the air. But with any sip of alcohol my body turns into a furnace, so I immediately resume my regularly scheduled walking sweat. The Piazza del Duomo isn't far. I can see a spire from the cathedral and we follow it until we reach the clearing. It's a pleasant night and many people are hanging out around the square. A couple of competing bands play at the restaurants surrounding. We stand and enjoy the lit cathedral for a moment before submitting to our exhaustion. Down to the Metro, we take the 10 minute ride north to Centrale.

At the hotel we collapse. The AC still isn't cooling properly, but by this point we could sleep in rain, sleet, snow, or sand storm. We hold off our good night's until we get our alarms set, and poof. We're out.

3: TO CORNIGLIA

I wake up early, around 7am, excited. At 9:20 we have tickets bound for Corniglia, the smallest of the five towns known as Cinque Terre. Talking with the handful of people we know who have been to Italy before, they all say the Cinque Terre is their favorite. I'm eager to get there, and also famously OCD about getting places early, so I shower off and pack up my few things.

Around 8am, I wake up Jennie. We've been required to become morning people thanks to becoming adults with real responsibilities (eww). But after a long day of travel and heat, I know it's best not to greet her first thing with too much enthusiasm. Especially before the first drip of coffee hits her. So a after a few smiles, kisses, and watch checks I head downstairs in search of breakfast while she showers and gets ready.

I wind down the stairwell and into the lobby, but no food or attendant is there. I poke my head back in the stairwell and spot a small sign pointing down into the basement. It didn't say anything about breakfast, but my stomach was growling so I decided to chance it. Down one flight, past the maintenance room, and through a dimly lit hallway I found the curiously placed breakfast area. It is stocked with pastries and a basket of fruit. I grab a few things and have a seat. Immediately a young girl comes over to ask if I would like an Americano or Cappuccino. She brings my drink and I eat quickly. Done, I grab a few things and start to head out of the small room. I hear quick footsteps behind me and rapid Italian followed by very broken English. I turn and the girl is fixed on me with angry eyes. I shrug, not understanding, and she walk over to the wall to another small sign. "No take food out." I debated tucking the food and running, but in the end I didn't feel the stale pastries worth the trouble. So I sit down the plate and she walks away. But, before heading up, I stash an orange in my pocket. Sometimes you just have to stick it to the man. Or in this case, the 14 year old girl.

Upstairs Jennie is all packed up and ready, so we set out for the station. We get there a touch early so we sit against the wall waiting for our platform to be called. When it's time, we stamp our tickets in the machine and board our assigned car. It's an old train, not lined with rows but instead with separated compartments. Flashes of the Hogwarts Express pop into my mind as we find an empty compartment and stow our bags overhead.

After a few minutes, a woman comes in with her three kids. She sits them down and in strongly accented English asks us to watch them while she runs to get water. Jennie and I look at each other in bewilderment, silently praying this woman has not just abandoned her kids on us. She returns after a couple of minutes filled with nervous sweats, thanks us, and issues orders to her kids.

Some older ladies peep into our cabin, and the mother explains that we are in their assigned seats. She points us down the hall to our ticketed seats, and we make ourselves comfortable in our new compartment. We are joined shortly by an Italian grandmother and her two grandkids. One is a tightly groomed toddler boy, the other an even younger girl. Another boy, older and alone, sits staring out the window. Finally, the whistle blows and we're on our way.

Heading south from Milan we pass through farm after farm. Rows of corn and stacked hay bales decorate our journey. Grandma, after enduring a few minutes of shirt sleeve tugging by the kids pulls out an iPad. The kids' eyes grow wide and they become lost in the technology. It's not long before the rhythm of the train lulls the little girl to sleep. She passes out on her brother's shoulder, and soon slips down flat against the seat.

About halfway in, the farmland gives way to steep mountains. Perhaps I should have studied up on the geography of Italy a bit better, because they take me completely off guard. For a minute I think we have boarded the wrong train and headed for the Alps. But I check the passing town names against my map and am reassured we are headed South to the coast.

The towns are carved into the mountains. It's beautiful and completely unexpected to see homes and church steeples back dropped by the rugged highland. Outside in the hall, the kids from our original compartment are yelling in high pitched voices the same words over and over again. "Ponte!" "Terraferma!" Every single bridge we crossed was "Ponte!" And when we made it back to land, "Terraferma!" Passing through the mountains, we crossed a bridge every thirty seconds. So this quickly began to annoy me. And while I don't necessarily approve of kids cramming their noses in technology all day every day, I certainly wish their mom was prepared like our now snoozing grandma with an iPad distraction.

Our train is running late, and we're already cutting it close for our connection in Genova when we make an extended stop at a station just a short ride from the city. When the train pulls out, they announce our next stop will be Genova Piazza Principe, our connection point. Suddenly, the cabin goes dark save a few very dim lights in the hall. We whiz into a tunnel at high speed and with one of the mountains sitting on top of us the pressure wreaks havoc on my ears. We stay in the tunnel for what feels like an hour, but is more like 10 minutes, before returning to the fresh open air.

It's already well after noon when we arrive in Genova, and our connection left at 11:30am. Our tickets are regional and can be used on any regional train (this is why validation is important, or travelers could easily reuse a ticket). We scan the daily schedule posted a paper on the wall and find a train leaving in an hour going to Vernazza, but not Corniglia. Vernazza is another one of the small towns in the Cinque Terre, so we figure going there will be fine. It is only one town over from Corniglia.

With a bit of time to kill, we step out of the station and onto the streets of Genova. The station isn't in the center of town, but there are still a few nice streets to meander. We end up stopping at a small shop for a hotdog. It's served sliced lengthwise and wrapped in a soft shell tortilla and smothered with sauce. Interesting, but tasty.

I can't speak for the rest of Genova, but this part certainly has a charm to it. Roads snake up into the mountains and the city feels nestled appropriately into the environment.

Back at the station we pile in with the crowd already formed on the platform. The train is, of course, running late. When it arrives, people push to get on before anyone can even exit causing a cluster of claustrophobia. Onboard, the seats are in rows alternating facing forwards and backwards, with an upstairs and downstairs. We sit downstairs, and after a stop are faced by a couple of girls our age, one Italian, one French, babbling on in English about the ineptitudes of their boyfriends.

In one of the countless long tunnels, our train screeches to a halt. This is terrible for so many reasons. It was already hot, but now with all air flow stifled it is suffocating. Everyone is sweating and miserable and smelly. Quite literally everyone on the train looks like they could pass out at any moment, except for one man in African styled clothes and headdress. He sits looking cool as a cucumber, perfectly unphased by the experience. After 20 minutes of no movement due to who knows what (breakdown? train heist? sleepy conductor?) we begin moving again with no explanation.

When we emerge from the tunnel we get our first glimpse of the Mediterranean. The view is incredible. Out of one window lush, green mountains rise high above us, and out of the other, the deep blue waters of the most storied sea on earth. We stop at every town along the coast, so it takes a couple of hours to finally reach Vernazza. But we get lost in the views and lose our worry of time.

Arriving in Vernazza, we search the time tables again for the next train stopping in Corniglia. There is one listed, but when a train pulls into the station it has no markings or indication of its destination whatsoever. A few minutes later when the next nondescript train pulls in we decide to hop on and cross our fingers. We stand holding onto a bar unsure of our decision. The train keeps speeding up and at this pace I have serious doubts it intends to stop. The sound of brakes screeching have never been more welcomed as the station signs outside read Corniglia. I feel like God may have just had mercy on our weary traveling souls and stopped the train for us as we were the only ones to exit. Either way, we were on "terraferma."

4 CORNIGLIA

Compared to the flood of tourists on the Vernazza platform, Corniglia is deserted. We exit the station onto the only road. The town is perched on a high cliff overlooking the sea and there are only two ways to get there. A bus totes tourists from the station up the winding road and into town. Or, there is a walking path which leads to switchback stairs up the cliffside. We've been cramped up in trains, so we veer left down the walking path.

A handful of people are walking down from the town, but nobody is walking with us. Corniglia is the smallest and least tourist-riddled of the Cinque Terre, and it's beginning to show. The path is elevated, with the train tracks below us on our left. And below the tracks, the sea. A salty breeze blows in from the water and the steep green mountains block the afternoon sun. It's a beautiful day.

At the end of the path, the switchback stairs start their way up. If you ever go to Corniglia I'd suggest not looking up. Just take the stairs as they come. Sneaking peaks at the 33 flights awaiting is not encouraging in any way.

About halfway up the stairs, a woman sits painting beautiful watercolors of the town and it's setting. We stop a bit to admire. She's sitting on the stone wall working on another. The colors are vibrant, drawing us in. At this point though, we are tired and sweaty and out of breath so we don't even discuss buying one. It's funny how little decisions and circumstances can really nag and bother. Because during our remaining time in the Cinque Terre, Jennie and I will pass the painter twice more and not say anything to each other. Later, in Rome as our trip winds down and we're looking for souvenirs and keepsakes to remember this amazing honeymoon, we'll both long to climb the stairs again just to buy one of the lady's watercolors.

At the top, we wind through the stony buildings in search of the main (only) town square. We booked a room with a woman named Sandra and were supposed to have arrived to meet at 2pm. But, with our missed train connection, it's now 4:30pm and she isn't in the cafe we had agreed to meet. There is only one alley through town, so we continue walking until we happen upon a small sign saying "Sandra Villas." We push the buzzer, but nobody comes. Another push and we here a man hollering from somewhere. I happen to look up, and an old Italian man in a white tank top is hanging out of the window.

"Umm… Sandra?" I say.

"No! Your name ok?" He responds.

I give him our name and he disappears for a couple of minutes. When he pops back out of the window he says Sandra isn't here, but someone will go find her. Then, a lady opens the door and with hand gestures tells us to wait here. She hurries off down the alley and returns shortly with keys. She instructs us to follow her to the room. Sandra will join us in a moment.

The lady is very nice and asks a few questions in poor English. I respond, but I'm not sure she catches even a word. Our room is just off the square. She opens the door to a small but clean space. Immediately my eyes are drawn to the window. When we booked this room the only pictures were of the bed and bathroom, so we figured the view wasn't much to write home about. Boy were we wrong. Rows and rows of vines lined the mountainside, which crashed almost violently down into the Mediterranean. Stunning.

As the lady shows us the keys, the towels, and the AC, another woman walks in.

"I wait for 2 hours in the cafe!" says who I assume to be Sandra.

"I'm very sorry our train was late." I respond, though I'm not sure Sandra or her helper could understand.

She goes on to say nearly everyone arrives late and it's quite alright. And they joke about us being silly for walking up all the stairs and that we should have waited on the bus. On the small vanity in the room she points out a few business cards of local places we should visit. She disappears for another minute and returns with beach towels, in case we go down to the water. We say our thanks and goodbyes, and the two ladies leave us.

A planned thirty minute nap turns into a two hour sleep. We take cold showers to wake us up, and head out to stroll the town. Turning left takes us to the few shops and restaurants, right takes us up a few steps through a tight alley leading to a cliffside overlook. We turn left in search of gelato and get some two scoops each from a dread-headed teenager.

Another day of travel without eating much leaves our tummies growling. At the corner of the gelato shop is a place called Dau Tinola. It sits facing the only actual street through Corniglia, a good place to people watch. We sit outside, next to an elderly woman and her small yappy dog. I order spaghetti drizzled with olive oil, herbs, and spices. This part of Italy is famed for its pesto, so Jennie goes for pesto pasta. While eating, we watch the locals as they begin their evening stroll. A few men pass with fishing nets thrown over their shoulders, disappearing down the cliffside.

The economy of the Cinque Terre used to rely almost exclusively on fishing and wine. Wine production is still big, but tourism has eroded most of the fishing industry, but Corniglia at least retains the fishing village charm.

Our plates are huge and at first we don't think there's any way we can finish them. But we just keep on eating. It'll become a common theme of the trip. It's impossible to eat enough food and drink enough water to stay fueled in the heat wave. After we finish and pay, we meander back up the street satisfied. The food was simple, but excellent.

We stop in to a little shop for a bottle of the local wine. The friendly and boisterous clerk recommends a white wine grown on the hill just across from our room. He points us to a cooler with the bottles chilled, and breaks us off some freshly made focaccia, drizzled with herbs and olive oil.

The sun is beginning to set as we walk on past our room and to the overlook. From here we can see Manarola and Monterosso al Mare, two of our neighboring towns. The sun sinks below the water and night falls as we sip wine and talk about how beautiful this place really is. The stars are incredible. Knoxville isn't the biggest or brightest city, but even on the outskirts there is enough artificial light to mute the stars. Here, there's nothing more than the occasional dim house light. We trace constellations and make imaginary plans to open a coffee shop/bed & breakfast here.

The next morning we are up and moving around 9am. Just outside our room is the cafe recommended by Sandra, Caffe Matteo. We stop in for a couple of coffees and croissants stuffed with chocolate. Before heading off, we grab a couple of waters to at least make an attempt at staying hydrated.

This morning our plan is to hike the mountain trail from Corniglia to Vernazza, about a 2.5 mile trip. We make our way to the start of the trail and the sun is already beating down on our necks. The path hugs the cliff and has beautiful views of the water. It dips down and then rises back up a number of times before we start to climb steadily up and over the crest of the mountain between the two towns. We stop a number of times, partly because the views of Corniglia are gorgeous, and partly because we are terribly out of shape.

Soon, a group catches up to us and we all play leapfrog with the lead. But, knowing we're only a mile or so in and hearing the couple behind us talking about their marathon running, we decide to hold up and let them walk on.

After 45 minutes of hard walking the "are we there yets" start. About that time, we come up on the only rest stop along the trail, a small bar hanging off the cliff. A few Americans are walking towards us giggling. The guy in the group waves and tells us the real view is on the other side of the bar, and that I ought to cover Jennie's eyes.

So we pass the bar, and a person that can only be described as an Italian male supermodel is repairing a stone terrace just below the path. He is scantily clothed and well-tanned, with long dark hair and piercing eyes. He's the kind of good looking that nobody can deny. I guess he is used to being oodled over, and he waves and shoots us a wink as he wipes off sweat. I ask Jennie if she thinks I could be a supermodel. She chuckles and humors me and we walk on.

Past the halfway point is mostly downhill. Jennie and I both have knees much older than they should be, so the strain is uncomfortable. Soon I start to get tired and careless and I roll my ankle. Jennie throws me over her shoulder and carries me the rest of the way (only kidding, of course). About an hour and half after we set off, we reach Vernazza

We approach Vernazza from the East and stop to take pictures from the trail looking down onto the town. As we take pictures a lady, Asian, alone, and strapped down with camera equipment and backpacks, keeps stepping in the way. Once or twice is understandable, as it's a small clearing on the path with only so many angles. But every single time we move she steps in. Jennie's temper begins to flare and I notice her pursed lips. I give her a hug and we sit and wait for her to leave before snapping some intruder free shots. Jennie doesn't take kindly to rudeness.

With wobbly knees we make our way down into town. We twist through a few shaded and cobbled alleys before spilling out onto the main avenue of Vernazza. We face a gelato shop, and take it as a sign to grab some lemon and strawberry yumminess and find a shady curb seat to rest our legs.

Being on the primary pedestrian path, we watch the cycle of tourists come and go. Each train drops off a new drove, who make their way down the street towards the sea. They replace earlier arrivals, who make their way slowly up the hill towards the train station. Images of ocean waves come to mind, an appropriate image I think.

The town itself is beautiful, a rainbow of tightly packed, sometimes disheveled buildings tucked into a small cove. Though its charm is slightly diminished by the sheer number of tourist groups. To our legs dismay, we force them to make carry us up a winding back alley to get another view from above the town. At the top of the alley, we come to a platform with a ticket desk. Apparently this view costs 10 euros a piece. The small Italian woman behind the desk looks near passing out from the heat. She is fanning herself in a daze. We step back and contemplate feigning ignorance and trying to just walk right by her. But when we raise our gaze to the lookout deck, it's packed. We decide it's not worth the trouble. No doubt the little Asian lady is up there butting her way into a thousand vacation memories, anyways.

Taking a different route down, we come out near the small beach at the end of the main street. We enjoy the ocean spray for a while as we take in the picturesque view featured on most Cinque Terre post cards. A stunning view, yes. But on the postcards the beach isn't overrun with yelling children. And the boats in the bay aren't tainted by their exorbitant pricing signs. 100 euros for a 30 minute ride? No thanks. I cannot fault the locals for capitalizing on the popularity, however. I only hope that they are the beneficiaries and not some tourism fat-cat from afar.

Back up the street, we decide to grab lunch. At a small but charming pizzeria, Jennie gets a giant slice of pizza with salami, and I decide on a sandwich loaded with greens. We get a large Coca-Cola to wash it down and wait like vultures for an arguing American couple to vacate the only bench in sight. We wait close enough to hear the two arguing over the guy's friends. She doesn't like them, one in particular, and she refuses to spend time with them that evening. He tries to defend them, but she isn't having any of it. She grabs her things and marches off, the guy following in defeat. I'm not usually one to be glad a couple are arguing. But in this case, Jennie and I really wanted that bench.

Just as the day before, the trains stopping in the station at Vernazza have no discernible markings, and the timetable is reliably inaccurate. We also realize that in order to ride the trains amongst the 5 tourist towns, you are supposed to buy the "Cinque Terre" card. The cards run anywhere from 5 to 50 euros, depending on the size of your group and how long it stays valid. Jennie and I discuss this, and decide there is no way someone on board could ever be checking tickets. The trains are crammed like a subway between the towns. So we decide to be rebellious and wing it without tickets.

We are hoping to reach Manarola, the town just to the

east of Corniglia. But the train we decide on has other ideas. It rages past Corniglia and Manarola and just as we think we're headed to all the way to the more distant city of La Spezia, it squeals to a halt in Riomaggiore, the easternmost town of the Cinque Terre.

At first glance, Riomaggiore has little going for it. We grab some vending machine water, and decide to take the Via dell' Amore, a quaint, cobbled ocean cliff walkway between Riomaggiore and Manarola. We scale the stairs only to find the path is closed for repairs. Back toward the station, we spot a small sign pointing toward a tunnel. A handful of tourists enter and we fall in line. We pass a few flute buskers, who I am amazed can withstand the heat and stale air in the tunnel. We emerge out the other side at the bottom of a staggeringly steep hill.

Slowly trudging upwards, we make our way past the hostels and tourist catering businesses. Perhaps at the tippy top of the street things become more charming. Or down a side street we didn't see. But this uphill part of town doesn't seem noteworthy.

At the base of the hill, you can take stairs down into the stonework and out into the bay area. The boats and cafes here are gorgeous, but it is very crowded and the sun is starting to beat so strongly that we don't last long. We enjoy the atmosphere for a bit before heading back through the tunnel and to the station.

The Riomaggiore train platform is small and jammed with people. I imagine a number of them were dropped off here by mistake and didn't even venture into town before switching rail sides. People are pushing, trying make their way to the counters and kiosks to buy a rail pass. We hop on the first train heading west, still passless.

The train zips past Manarola, Corniglia, Vernazza, and finally stops at Monterosso al Mare. Monterosso is the beach resort option of the Cinque Terre. We decline to leave the station area, and wait another 20 minutes for a train heading east. At this point, we have no idea where we'll end up. We're still trying to get to Manarola, but when the train screeches just in time to stop at Corniglia, we get off fearing we'll never make it back to our base town if we don't seize this chance.

Since we leave the next day for Florence, we go ahead and buy our tickets at the kiosk. We'll arrive in Florence by way of La Spezia and Pisa. Heading up the cliffside stairs is daunting, but we have caught our second wind and make quicker work of them. About half-way up an American couple is panting and cursing. They determine the climb isn't worth it, a decision quite a few travelers reach. I try to convince them to continue up, but they aren't having it. They head down and we press on.

Reaching the top we are reminded of Corniglia's quiet charm. The climb and infrequent shuttle service keeps the tourist traffic down. A few travelers stroll the alley and peep into the cafes. But we've left the droves of family vacations and tours behind.

Getting back to our room, we phone home and I take a cold shower to wash off the heat and stink. The beating sun left Jennie and I both red and tired. A quick recharge with a nap gets us ready for the evening.

After the midday heat breaks into evening, we head back out for a stroll through the town. To walk from end to end is about 15 minutes, so the stroll is mercifully short on our aching legs. We get some gelato and some kind of Italian craft beer and find a bench street side. The few tourists left make their way out of town by foot or shuttle. Fishermen head down towards the sea, and the townspeople begin to walk about.

For supper, we head back to the inner piazza near our room for a patio table at Caffe Matteo. I get a wild hair to try something new, so I get the smoked swordfish salad. It is strong and fishy, but fresh and full of flavor. I scarf it down and manage to steal a couple of bites of Jennie's gnocchi with ragu sauce. The gnocchi is borderline divine.

After our meal, we head to a shop where the owner directs us to another local wine, this one by a different family. We thank him, and head back to our room to enjoy it with our private view of the vines. We're both exhausted and burnt, but so happy. And so in love!

5: TO FLORENCE

We wake up with sun rays shooting into our window, with a couple of stretches and yawns to prepare us for the day. We pack up and head back over to Caffe Matteo for some much needed caffeine and fuel. We both get a chocolate croissant and wash them down with cappuccinos.

Going down the stairs, we realize just how wobbly our legs are. Our geriatric joints whinnie with every step. We're plenty early, so we take our time and enjoy the views as we go.

At the station, we check the timetable to see that our 8:53 train to La Spezia has been cancelled. We'll have to wait around until the 9:33 train arrives. A nervous looking older couple is pacing on the platform. Jennie and I are hesitant to make conversation with them, as they look out of sorts about something, presumably the train schedule. But with nearly an hour to kill, I greet them with a "howdy."

The couple is from Pennsylvania. They've visited Italy as a side trip, after coming to Europ to see their daughter who married a Frenchman and lives in Paris. They're connecting on our same train in La Spezia to Pisa, and they're up in arms over the delay. "What if we miss our train? We'll surely miss our flight!" I try to ease their minds reminding them nothing on Italy is on time. I'm sure our connection in La Spezia will be late just the same. I can see them squinting at my lips, no doubt to decipher my southern accent.

By the time the 9:33 train arrives a few more tourists have joined us. It's a short trip to La Spezia, and when we pull into the station Jennie and I immediately make for our connecting platform. We're followed from our train car by another young couple from America. Our train is (surprise!) running late. So we fall into conversation with the couple.

They live in Boston, where the girl is from. The guy is aussie. They are on a 21 day trip hitting Rome, Paris, London, and Glasgow. They're taking trains through Italy before renting a car to head North. We exchange train stories and they tell us about the hellish heat in Rome. They say Rome had the highest temperatures of recorded history while they were there with no signs of it breaking anytime soon. Jennie and I exchange glances and have a conversation in our head:

"Dear lord, surely it can't get any hotter than we've already faced..."

"I hope not, I'm already sweaty and smelly enough."

We're starting to lull back to sleep when our train for Pisa arrives. Onboard Jennie catches up on pop culture with a *People* magazine. From the cover, I read that Channing Tatum is going to let his daughter watch Magic Mike when she grows up. In a stroke of honesty, he says he is saving money for the therapy she'll need afterwards.

We share our car with a young Asian couple, and an extremely talkative Italian granny. The girl is eating half a melon, spitting seeds as discreetly as possible. And the nerdiest thing I'll see all trip award goes to the guy she is with, who is watching a mathematics lecture with hilariously oversized headphones.

La Spezia looks very industrial. As we zip in and out of tunnels, the talkative granny loses reception on her cell phone and quickly redials. We pass warehouses and plants with smoke towers, cranes and shipping crates.

Our train car is like a viewing room for stereotypes. An Italian gesturing wildly in passionate conversation, Asians in anime shirts watching math lectures, and Americans reading celebrity gossip. In other news, it's apparently shark week on TV back home.

Our train hugs near the coastline on its way to Pisa, but the coastal views aren't at all attractive. Scenes of run-down industry block us from the Mediterranean. Inland, however, is beautiful. Steep, jagged mountains carve through the landscape. Towns, churches, and convents are tucked into the mountain valleys.

The mountaintops look snowcapped. Either our eyes are being deceived, or someone forgot to tell the mountains there's a serious heat wave going on. Later, I'll research and discover that we rode along the Apuan Alps, famous for their marble rock and quarries. I'd imagine what we thought was white snow, was actually the beginnings of a floor tile or countertop.

As we pull into Pisa, Granny puts on a pair of aviator sunglasses that would cost $500 back home. Italian style is real. Everyone quickly exits and piles on the train leaving immediately for Florence. Every single car is packed. We quickly check the departure schedule and find there's a train leaving for Florence every 20 minutes or so. We decide to wait, and head to the next labeled platform. The train arrives early and it throws us for a loop. We hesitantly get on and find a seat. Hardly anyone is on board, and not many others get on. We're afraid we've hopped on the wrong train, and just as we're about to go for the door the train takes off. The intercom crackles and we half expect the speaker to tell us we're headed off to some far-flung town, but we hear Firenze (Florence), and settle back into our seats.

We rub our aching calves and look at the pictures we've taken so far. Jennie bought us some Nutella filled cracker bars at the station, and we devour them. As the ride goes on, we start to see a most idyllic Tuscan landscape. Skinny trees line winding roads. The terrain has smoothed into rolling vineyards and farms. This is the Italy seen on romance films and travel shows.

A train employee comes by and cleans our car and Jennie remarks at how clean the train actually is. Most American's wouldn't think twice before dropping a wrapper in the floor, but there is none of that here. I don't think I've seen a speck of trash on any of the trains we've been on. The train cleaner moves through emptying waste bins and wiping down seats.

The houses and estates we pass are full of color. Yellows, greens, pinks all merge together to brighten the hills. In the distance, we see a large stone villa surrounded by hedges and small trees. "Behold!" I say. "The original Olive Garden!" Jennie cracks a smile and laughs, though I'm not sure if it's with me or at me.

The train attendant walks through our car a couple of times as we enter the outskirts of Florence. With each pass my nerves start to grow. We forgot to validate our tickets in Pisa. I didn't see a machine while we were on the platform. It wasn't until we were about to hop off and the doors closed in front of us that we saw one hanging on a column just ahead. I make Jennie practice batting her eyelashes in case we are checked, but luckily the attendant never pays us any attention.

6: FLORENCE

We disembark in the bustling Stazione di Santa Maria Novella, and head out and across the street. We can already see Il Duomo over the rooftops. Our apartment we booked is right next to Il Duomo, so we are glad to know we'll have a landmark to guide us as we explore. It's around 1pm and we are to meet our hostess at the front door of the apartment building at 4, so we find a restaurant to tuck into for a bit and enjoy some lunch.

I'm a bit odd, and don't like cheese. So I'm ecstatic to see a marinara pizza on the menu at La Dantesca Pizzeria. Jennie and I share the huge pizza covered in sauce, olive oil, and tons of yummy spices. Jennie loves cheese, but she's a good sport about sharing. We make short work of the pizza and dive back into the city streets.

The atmosphere is electric. Even in the sweltering heat, the city bursts with romance and vibrancy. This cradle of the Renaissance looks captured in time, as though a member of the Medici family could turn the corner in feathered hat at any moment. Every street we look down seems to tell a story. For a history nerd, Florence is earthly paradise.

We walk into the Piazza del Duomo and what many describe as the world's most beautiful cathedral rises before us. It's a vast gothic structure. The exterior is decorated with pink, green, and white marble. But the star of the show is the incredible dome. When Filippo Brunelleschi proposed the dome in the 15th century he was thought to be insane. Nothing of the size and span of the dome had been completed in modern history. Brunelleschi studied old building techniques, and had to invent entirely new lifting and scaffolding techniques in order to construct the double nested dome. The building process was filled with controversy and peril. But the result is arguably the most iconic structure of the Renaissance.

Turning out of the piazza, we make our way down the Via di Servi, where our apartment is located. We pass up our meeting spot, and end up in a cafe/bar to cool off with a couple of beers and some cheese to make up for Jennie's lactose-free lunch. Close to 4pm, we wait outside what we think is the entrance to our apartment building. We put our backs on the huge, old wooden doors. They probably reach 15 or 20 feet tall and are solid. After a few minutes a woman walks toward us with intention. Our host Cristina greets us and shows us in. I was hoping she'd give us one of those old iron keys, but the locks have been modernized. From the building lobby, we head up the elevator a few floors and then up a flight of stairs to the roof.

As soon as we cross out onto a terrace the view staggers us. Our apartment building is maybe 50 yards from Il Duomo, and it looks like we could reach out and touch the dome's roofing. Our entrance is on the terrace, with a window looking out directly at the massive structure. It's breathtakingly beautiful.

There's a full kitchen, living room, washer, large bathroom, and cozy bedroom in the apartment. Traditional tile flooring, thick wood beams, and the view make us want to ship our stateside belongings and call this home forever.

There is a stationary below the window looking out at Il Duomo, and I sit and take notes while Jennie takes stock of the place and rests her feet for a bit.

As the sun begins to hide behind the low skyline, we go in search of gelato. In researching Florence, I had read about a heavenly gelato shop called Vivoli. It is a few blocks over, and a couple up from our apartment. There, we have trouble choosing, and both get two scoops. Both of us got a scoop of the chocolate mousse, and we both want to swim in its opulence. It's so good that a few hours later when I'm taking notes on our day, neither of us can even recall the other flavor we chose. We vow to return before leaving for more.

Jennie and I both enjoy cooking, and eating out every meal has begun to wear on us. So in between Vivoli and our apartment we plan to stop into a grocery store for dinner supplies. As we head that direction a woman in all white robes and headdress, along with white face chalk approaches. Florence is notorious for its gypsies and thieves, so I quickly become vigilant and protective. She holds out her hand and walks towards us begging for money. I quickly fend her off, grab Jennie and quickstep down another street. Annoying, but even a creepy woman in white-face can't bring down our mood after that chocolate mousse.

We come upon a small grocery shop called Conad. My inner child can't help but make a few gonads jokes as we walk in. The store isn't very wide, but is forever long. We buy some fresh pasta from the counter, some olive oil, veggies, and some regional Chianti before heading to the apartment.

Back under the shadow of the dome, I begin chopping tomato, onion, zucchini, and garlic and set a pot of water to boil. I toss the veggies and sauté, but when we turn on the oven to toast some bread the main breaker gives out.

Cristina had warned us not to use many things at once as the system can't handle the load, but it still seems crazy to me that a nice apartment in a first world country can't handle running an oven and the AC unit at the same time. Nevertheless, we turn off the AC and a couple of lights and I go in search of the breaker.

Jennie takes over cooking duties while I head to the basement of the building to find the electrical system. From the ground floor lobby, there is an old, withered door leading down into the basement, but it is locked. My room key doesn't work on it, so I trudge back upstairs in search of the proper key. Back downstairs with the key in hand I unlock the door and walk down the dangerously steep stairs. It takes me a minute to decipher the system and find a way to reset the breaker, but I finally get it on again.

By the time I get back upstairs the power has already kicked off again. But the food is ready, so we sit down in the dark and try to eat while the food is hot. After a few bites, a guy pecks on our window. He can see us eating. With our power off, the Wi-Fi in our apartment is also off. Apparently, his family uses our Wi-Fi and this has greatly disrupted his evening. He gestures wildly and claims we must go down and fix this. Now.

I want to explain he is disrupting a nice meal on our honeymoon, but between his faltering English and my nonexistent Italian I give in and trudge back down to flip the switch. This time the power stays on. With the Wi-Fi working, we finish up our meal and enjoy our wine looking out at the dome in peace.

We wake up the next day a bit late, and it's a little after 9am when we get our start. Our travel worn bodies may have slept longer if it weren't for the screaming kid next door. If I see the window pecker, I'll be sure to point out that our Wi-Fi has nothing to do with his terribly obnoxious toddler.

We make our way around the Piazza del Duomo. The line to enter the cathedral is forever long, and going in isn't tops on our list so we decline with the intention of checking another time. The Battistero di San Giovanni, the baptistery in the piazza, is covered with scaffolding undergoing a preservation attempt.

Off the piazza, we snake through a few alleys. Sculptures and frescoes dot the corners and buildings. The city streets alone are worthy of an art museum title. We turn onto a main thoroughfare, and immediately I see another white-faced woman in her robes. She is marching up to people demanding a handshake. We watch as she attempts it on a few people, and even see her slip her hand into a couple of pockets. We keep good distance from her as we stroll in the crowd.

The street leads us into the city's heart, the Piazza della Signoria. We gaze at the architecture of the buildings, and are drawn into the corner of the Piazza to the Palazzo Vecchio. It's the town hall, and outside there is a copy of the famous Statue of David. There is also a large fountain with a statue of Neptune. As we are admiring the craftsmanship, another white-face lady marches right towards us. I put my hand up in the universal stop motion, shake my head, and try to look intimidating. Either I looked mean, or we looked poor, because the woman immediately turns and heads for another victim. I have since read that the white-faced ladies work together, and use the white chalk to mark people they discover are easy targets. There isn't a lot of information out there about them, and what little I could find is speculation. But I know one thing for sure, they are creepy, and I don't like them.

From the Piazza della Signoria, we cross over a few streets to the riverside. The Arno River is spanned by the Ponte Vecchio, one of the most famous bridges in the world. It was originally occupied by butcher shops, which hang off the side of the stonework. In modern times the butcher shops have been replaced with jewelers and businesses catering to the tourists. Still, looking at the Ponte Vecchio from the Ponte Santa Trinita, a bridge a few hundred yards to the west, I can imagine carts and townspeople scattered about in daily affairs.

We snap a few pictures with the Ponte Vecchio in the background before crossing over to the southern side of the Arno. There aren't nearly as many tourists filling the streets on this side, but the buildings maintain the same central town charm.

The sun starts to beat on us with midday intensity, so we decide to break for lunch. In a small 4 table cafe south of the river we enjoy a fresh meal. I have Penne cooked in a chianti wine and meat sauce. Jennie gets a traditional spaghetti, both are wonderful.

Before walking back to the north side, we make a point to view the Palazzo Pitti. Once the residence of ambitious town banker Luca Pitti, the massive and severe looking structure also served as a power base for Napoleon, and even an Italian royal palace. Now the enormous building has been converted into a museum.

We sit in the courtyard admiring and hydrating for a while. Kids are kicking around a ball over the cobblestones. I marvel at the fact that there is no graffiti. Along the walls that contain the rail system we've seen some. But I've not seen the first marking on any of the historic building. Is there a respect for the past that keeps hoodlums from spraying block letters everywhere? Or maybe they use Renaissance era torture techniques on people caught to discourage it.

Crossing back over the Arno on the Ponte Vecchio, we follow an elevated walkway above us back to the heart of town. The walkway was built by the moneybags of developing Florence as a private pathway from the Palazzo Vecchio, over top of the Ponte Vecchio, and ending at the

Palazzo Pitti. It was constructed so they might avoid the common folk below, and reportedly the smell of the butcher shops on the bridge.

The Uffizi Gallery is filled with works by Raphael, Michelangelo, Caravaggio, Da Vinci, etc. The line, unfortunately, is around the corner and down the street. We would like to see the famous artwork, but to us, the city itself is much more delightful and interesting than halls of hushed rooms with paintings. So we walk across the long, narrow courtyard of the Uffizi, back into the Piazza della Signoria.

The doors to the Palazzo Vecchio have opened, so we enter to find beautiful frescoes painted on the walls. The powerful Medici family once brought in rulers and aristocrats from around the known world to a festival and celebration to display Florence's greatness. The family commissioned frescoes of the faraway lands to indicate their power's reach. The frescoes survive today, large and detailed inside the palace.

With quite a bit of walking behind us, we decide it's time to reward ourselves with some gelato. More accurately, we decides it's past time to indulge in Vivoli's chocolate mousse gelato. We head northeast from the Piazza della Signoria, not looking at a map but using our natural attraction to yummy treats. We zig-zag down a few small streets, and know that we are getting close by spotting a few signs pointing to familiar landmarks.

A wrong turn leads us out into a large square. The Piazza Santa Croce and it's large basilica take us by surprise. Reflecting after our trip, the thing we loved most about Florence was the inability to take a wrong turn. Around every corner hid a beautiful church, or statue, or fresco, or fountain. Just to the left of the Basilica Santa Croce is a large statue of famed Florentine Dante Alighieri, whose Divine Comedy shaped not only world literature (and continues to do so), but also the entire Italian language. At the time of his writing, the language itself was fractured into hundreds, some believe thousands, of distinct dialects. He set out to write his Divine Comedy in a way that it could be read by all social classes. The result, a mixture of Tuscan and other regional dialects, along with elements of traditional Latin, lead Dante to be crowned "The Father of the Italian Language."

My linguistics geek-out calmed, Jennie and I retreated back the way we had come before, and turned down another street. We spot the Vivoli Gelato sign, and our pace increases with anticipation. We are both tempted to swim in a double scoop of chocolate mousse richness, but I pair the mousse with strawberry, and Jennie complements it with a coffee flavor. Savoring every bite, we head slowly back to our apartment to rest our legs and enjoy the beautiful terrace view.

With energy anew, we head back out into town as the sun begins to ease. We get distracted as soon as we turn the corner into the Piazza del Duomo by a Lindt Chocolate store. A rainbow of shiny truffle wrappers fill bins all around the shop. "It's our honeymoon, right?!?" we say to ourselves as we make our way around and fill up a bag each.

Towards the train station to buy our tickets for the next day's trip to Siena, we stop into a few book stores as an excuse to unwrap a truffle. A 10 minute walk turns into an hour long stroll looking at old leather bound notebooks and eating a variety of flavors. Eventually we make it to the station to secure tickets for the morning.

We take a different route on the way back to see the Basilica di San Lorenzo. This, another of the huge basilicas dotting the landscape of Florence, was the parish of the Medici family. It's interior was decorated by Donatello, Michelangelo, and Brunelleschi. The concentration of artwork and architecture in this city continues to blow us away. Jennie and I both lament the lack of craftsmanship in our modern American cookie cutter buildings and homes.

A few blocks south of the Basilica di San Lorenzo we make our way to our last destination before heading for supper. The Piazza della Repubblica is a massive city square. It sits on the site of a Roman forum, and later served as a ghetto before being rejuvenated during the time Florence served as the capital of a united Italy. Now, hip and expensive cafes line the edges, and a small carnival is set up in the middle of the square for kids to enjoy. A triumphant arch rises above us inscribed: "The ancient center of the city restored from age-old squalor to new life." It's hard for us to imagine the beauty of Florence every floundering in squalor.

Our stomachs signal us for supper. We cross a few streets and make our way through smaller alleys. Our nose leads us to a small restaurant with a tables on a small square. I get the Polpette alla Fiorentina (Meatballs smothered in a tomato and spinach sauce) and Jennie decides on Ravioli stuffed with mushrooms and cheese. Both meals are sensational and we devour them in no time. We enjoy the atmosphere of the patio on the square so we order a bottle of red wine and relax for a while. The couple behind me share a bistecca fiorentina, a huge hunk of steak served jarringly rare. But they cut through it like butter and finish every single bite.

Night has fully covered us and we retreat back to the apartment to read, write, and reflect. For street strollers like ourselves, Florence is doable in 2 days. But if you were to explore a few of the popular museums or basilicas, you could easily get lost in the artwork for weeks. Just take care to avoid the white-faced ladies.

7: TO SIENA

We've got some time before a train departs, so we stop into Caffe Moka across from the station for some fuel. We get 2 small coffees, and are charged 10 Euros! Getting charged 3 times the going Starbucks rate for subpar coffee is not a good start to the day.

In Stazione di Santa Maria Novella, we search the boards for our train. Platform 4, it says, so we set out looking but the platform is nowhere to be found. Finally, we spot a sign about 200 yards down one of the walks and give it a shot. Platform 4 must be for the outcast or smelly trains, because it's a good ways away from everything else in the station.

Jennie settles in with famed author Bill Bryson's *Neither Here Nor There*. It tells of his travels through Europe, as he retraces a similar trip from his younger years. This gets us thinking about taking a trip of our own through the continent. We talk about travel routes, the amount of pre-planning we'd do, expenses, if/how we'll make money, and how in the world we'll tell our parents we're going to live from a backpack for a few months or maybe even a year. I'm fairly certain my dad, famously cautious and worriesome, wouldn't sleep for the duration of our trip.

The train to Siena retraces half-way back to Pisa, turning south at a town called Empoli. A train attendant mopes his way into our mostly empty car. His entrance is like that of a Dementor from Harry Potter. He sucks the very life and happiness out of the space. He looks miserable, like he positively hates all living, breathing things. Luckily we validated our ticket, so we show him and don't have to face any more interaction with the poor man.

The route from Empoli to Siena passes through the occasional small town and hilltop villa. The ride is mostly farmland and sunflower fields. As we slowly roll through Castelfiorentino, an old man in a wheelchair is riding down the middle of the street blocking traffic from passing. Jennie and I laugh, joking about the old man protesting these confounding new cars blazing up and down the streets and ruining his town with noise and pollution.

As we draw closer to Siena, farms turn to vineyards. Nearly every hilltop is adorned by the kind of villa you see in movies. A couple of times we pass large, walled castles. Italy has beauty and history in excess it seems.

8: SIENA

Siena is a Tuscan hill town first settled by the Etruscans. Arriving by train puts you at the bottom of the steep hillside. Fortunately, Siena has become a quite popular tourist destination spurring the development of a long escalator system from the train station to the town gates. Emphasis on the word *long*. After passing through the few shops in the station we step onto the escalator and rise up for what seems like hours. Finally, we trade the stale enclosed air for fresh as we step out from the top platform into the street.

The sun is beaming, and atop the tall hill we feel like we're 5 feet from the surface. Turning left towards town, we are quickly drawn to a panoramic view of Tuscany. Villas, churches, and those iconic cypress trees spread into the horizon. We drop our packs and gaze at our surroundings in awe. Another American family joins us, and we take turns snapping photos for each other.

Strapping back on our packs, we head down the street and pass through the city gates. Large and looming brick walls still surround the city. Few cars are allowed on the streets within the walls, making Siena infinitely more quiet than Florence.

It's Sunday, and most of the shops are closed. Everything about Siena speaks to a Medieval charm. Nearly all of the buildings are constructed with the reddish-brown brick typical of the period. Even the doors, massive and wooden, appear to be unchanged since Medieval times.

As we walk mostly alone through the streets towards the main square, we start to see colored flags hanging from all of the buildings. The city is divided into 17 "contrade", or districts. These districts were set up in the Middle Ages in order to supply troops to the many military companies that were hired to defend Siena as it fought to defend its independence from Florence and other nearby city states. As time has gone by, however, the contrade have lost their administrative and military functions and have instead become simply areas of localized patriotism, held together by the emotions and sense of civic pride of the residents. Their roles have broadened so that many important events – baptisms, deaths, marriages, church holidays, sporting victories, even wine or food festivals – are celebrated only within one's own contrada.

These 17 contrade compete in the Palio de Siena. The Palio is a horse race held twice a year, July 2 and August 16. Ten horses and riders dressed in the appropriate colors, represent ten of the seventeen contrade. A pageant, the Corteo Storico, precedes the race, which attracts visitors and spectators from around the world.

The race itself, in which the jockeys ride bareback and circle the Piazza del Campo, usually lasts no more than 90 seconds. It is common for a few of the jockeys to be thrown off their horses while making the treacherous turns in the piazza, and indeed, it is not unusual to see unmounted horses finishing the race without their jockeys. Perhaps the horses, too, are antagonistic to their rival contrades.

We enter the Piazza del Campo in the center of the city and it is easy to see why it's regarded as one of the greatest Medieval town squares in Europe. The center portion of the square is laid brick, and is surrounded by spaced pylons marking the outer path on which the Palio takes place. The Piazza itself is shell-shaped, and is sloped down to a center point for drainage.

Standing in the Piazza del Campo is breathtaking, yes, but the midday sun again forces us to seek a shady lunch spot. We break away from the touristy center of town and walk a few blocks down Via Pantaneto. We are ushered to a table at small pizzeria by a lively and waddling character. He is singing, and the few locals at the tables occasionally chime in. I get a pizza marinara, and Jennie decides to try a pizza with smoked salmon. Both are delicious and we finish them off in record time, washed down with some kind of prosecco served by the singing owner mid high note.

We sit for a bit before taking a different street back towards the town center. Down a backstreet, we spot a tiny alleyway marked by a stone archway and iron gate. We walk over and look down to see dark twists and turns. Not a soul is around, and the path looks completely untouched since Medieval times. I open the gate and walk in, but Jennie is hesitant. There's a small sign hanging next to the archway. "What if it says 'will shoot tourists' or something?" she says. I laugh and hold out my hand and convince her to follow me through the gate.

Vines hang from the rooftops and fall onto the walls on either side of the tight path. We pass through a few more stone arches and we can hear the echoes of local families dining together. A window is open at ground level and an old Italian woman is in her kitchen cooking up a meal. As we walk on, we almost feel swallowed by the history of the path we're on. There are small wooden doors, maybe 5 feet tall carved into the stone with old iron hinges. They look like they haven't been opened in ages. I'd love to be able to open them and explore the mysteries they hold.

We've got some time before we meet Donato, our host, to be shown to our apartment. Back in the Piazza del Campo we find a shady spot in the center of the square and rest on our packs. In the piazza, eyes are immediately drawn to the Palazzo Pubblico and its tower. The tower was said to be built to the same height as the Siena Cathedral as a sign that the church and the state had equal amounts of power. The facade of the palace building itself is curved slightly inwards, reflecting the shell shape of the piazza. The result is a unique and visually stunning town square.

We meet Donato at a gelato shop a short walk from the apartment. We enter our building from a small square uphill from the main piazza. We take an elevator to the top floor, and then make our way up some steps to our door.

The view is breathtaking. Our apartment window overlooks the rooftops down into the Piazza del Campo. Beyond the piazza we can look out onto the towers, churches, and Tuscan countryside. We have been incredibly fortunate and spoiled with our views.

We unpack a few things and Jennie takes a quick nap while I contact our host in Rome about our upcoming stay. After a few minutes I wake Jennie up excited. She rubs her eyes and has that "this better be good" look on her face. I point her over to the window and we look out to see a most peculiar parade. Below us the different districts are displaying their colors. There is a purple team dancing on flatbed trucks, and a green team dressed up in sumo suits. Marching bands in competing colors are playing. A yellow team streaks through the center of the square and disappears down a side street. The parade circles a few times before also making its way down a side street.

We go down the stairs and elevator and out into the town once again. We can hear the parade begin to dissipate in the distance. We have intentions of cooking a meal in our apartment kitchen, but are quickly shot down by the Sunday evening shop closings. In retreating to our small square, we find there is a restaurant facing our apartment building that smells enticing. We enter and are pleasantly surprised to find a large stone room romantically lit with candles and white tablecloth. Wood beams show overhead, with a delicate candle chandelier hanging from the center beam. The restaurant, like the rest of Siena we had seen, looks unaffected by time.

I get a wild boar pasta, and Jennie devours a plate of ravioli with ricotta and truffles (of the mushroom variety, not chocolate). We hear the parade pick back up again in the square, and return to our window view to watch with a bottle of wine. We play cards and look out at the night sky before settling in for a good night's sleep.

We are startled awake early Monday morning by construction on the rooftop just outside our window. We dress quickly and make our way away from the hammering and sawing. Our first visit of the day is to the Duomo di Siena which sits only about 50 yards uphill from our building. It was purposefully built a good ways outside of the main square as a reminder of the separation of church and state. This idea and symbology was revolutionary for the time, as nearly all other cathedrals were built at the heart of their cities.

In the shadow of the Duomo, we stop to put sunscreen on Jennie's tomato red neck. In the distance we see the Basilica of San Domenico and decide to make our way over to it. We stop in a cafe along the way and sit for a coffee and croissant. The barkeep is a behemoth of a man, with only slight exaggeration I'd say at least 6'8" and 300 lbs. We be sure to thank him profusely as we leave. We climb and descend a few hills before coming to the Basilica.

The views looking back on the town center are beautiful. The basilica itself is much more simply adorned than the rest of the churches we have seen. Unfortunately, most of the outside is covered in scaffolding for restoration. But the doors are open so we enter to view the sanctuary. The inside is also simply adorned. We are drawn to the Chapel of Saint Catherine along the wall. A few locals are sitting in prayer. Just to the side of the chapel in a casing we spot the preserved finger of the saint, and quickly pedal away queasy. I'll never understand the Catholic's affinity for relics like preserved fingers.

Outside, we trudge up a dreadful hill back to the Piazza del Campo. We enter the Palazzo Pubblico and pay to tour the inside. Nearly every major room in the palace contains frescoes. These were unusual for the time in that they were commissioned by the governing body of the city, rather than by the Church or by a religious fraternity. They are also unusual in that many of them depict secular subjects instead of the religious subjects which are overwhelmingly typical of Italian art of this era.

We read a brief history of the city on a plaque in the basement. Siena was decimated by the Black Death in 1348. Approximately half the population died in the plague. The republic's economy was destroyed and the state quickly declined from its position of prominence in Italy. The Franciscan religious order rose to power in the city. The stagnation over the following centuries meant that while Siena did not develop during the Renaissance as did other Italian cities, it was also preserved both from bombardment during World War II and from modern development. This leaves us with the wonderful time-capsule town Siena is today.

Back in the main hall of the Palazzo Pubblico, we consider walking to the top of the tall tower. But when we discover we have to pay extra just to walk up the steps (no elevator) we decline. The view from our apartment window is better anyway.

We take lunch in a bustling small family restaurant in a square a few streets over. A mother and son seem to be the only employees. We are seated by the son, before being moved to a different table by the mother. The son apologizes and gives us complimentary drinks to repay. The son runs from table to table taking orders and fetching refills. My spaghetti with eggs and bacon has little of either, and Jennie's risotto is terribly salty. This is our first taste of disappointment, and I'm pretty sure the son can tell. As we leave, he apologizes again and again and asks us to come back for supper. Slim chance.

We mosey around a bit before getting some gelato. Jennie pouts because I order what she wants. More often than not, we share the same brain and thoughts. So we end up passing one waffle cone back and forth. We stop into a small grocer and pick up some prosecco and hair conditioner for Jennie before heading back to the apartment for a quick nap. Thankfully, the construction has stopped when we arrive.

In the evening we get hungry early thanks to our lackluster lunch. So we settle on a quick takeout place just off the Plaza del Campo. I get a laughably large croissant with a hotdog and french fries stuffed in the middle. The idea is novel and actually doesn't taste terrible. Jennie gets a single slice of pizza that's larger than her head and we have a seat in the center of the piazza to eat.

We enjoy the setting so we stay in the piazza to people watch. Most tourists make a day trip of Siena on tour busses so the square is filled with mostly locals as the day draws to a close. Families play, couples lay back with a bottle of wine, and school-age kids walk around pointing and giggling. We watch as a little girl, maybe 3 or 4 years old, runs a few yards away from her dad and turns around grinning. The dad holds out his arms and she rushes back over to him and jumps into his arms before repeating.

Back up in the apartment, we play gin rummy overlooking the town. Tonight the stars are out and the sky is amazing. We try to debate which window view has been the best, Corniglia's seaside vineyard, Florence's historic dome, or Siena's medieval square and countryside.

We sleep in the next morning, exhausted from the trip thus far. We rest in the apartment during the morning, reading about the town. I read something about the Basilica of San Domenico that throws me off. "Did you see anything about Saint Catherine's head being on display yesterday babe?" I ask Jennie.

"YES! OH MY GOSH!!!!!" She exclaims and immediately jumps up. "I saw it! I saw it! I thought I was crazy because you didn't say anything or even act like it was there. So I didn't say anything about it!"

We both immediately agree that we have to go back and inspect. We set out for the day, grabbing a quick lunch. On the way to the Basilica we take a detour to see an old Franciscan church and to get some more gelato.

In the Basilica of San Domenico, we stride immediately over to the Chapel of Saint Catherine. Jennie points straight ahead, and sure enough, tucked into the center of the chapel wall is a glass casing with a small pedestal. Presumably Saint Catherine's head stares out at onlookers. How on earth could I have missed this? We look morbidly for a moment before backing away. We walk out of the sanctuary, passing the saint's encased finger once again.

Walking away from the town center, we find ourselves approaching the Fortezza Medicea. The fort was built in the 1500s and has long since been demilitarized. It now has gardens atop its walls and an amphitheater and festival space inside. We find our way into the fort, and to the top of the surrounding walls. The gardens and hedges are pretty, and we find a bench with a view facing the city to rest our legs, enjoy a few sips of sugary drink to stave off our growing lethargy, and marvel at the view. 2 older men nearby are reading the paper and talking about life. Back home old men meet at the local Hardee's to do this. I prefer the Italian way.

Making our way back into town, we stop into a grocery store for some ingredients. We have decided to have a low-key night in order to recharge as best we can before heading for Rome at 6am the next morning. At the apartment, we crank the AC and rest ourselves. After a nice supper of chicken and veggies with tons of Italian herbs, we call it an early night.

9: TO ROME

We awake around 5am. We throw on our packs and head out into a crisp morning air. It feels nice not to start sweating instantly when we step outside. We pass through the Piazza del Campo one last time before making for the main gate. We descend the endless escalators to the station and grab some coffee from one of the small shops. Walking out on the platforms, we see our train has arrived early and start walking towards it. It gives a few beeps and the doors close when we're still 50 feet away. I run towards it without a plan, am I going to pry its doors open or what? The train pulls forward a little ways, stops, and opens its doors. Shew, Jennie and I board and sit on the platform for a few minutes before it pulls out of the station.

The train is very small, more like a shuttle. We have a connection in a town called Chiusi with a few hours to kill there. Just when we settle in for the ride, a girl comes running down the aisle and starts rapidly firing questions at us in Italian. We shrug at her… "Ummm, English or Español?" I ask her. She fires us a pissy look and marches on to question someone else.

The train cruises through the countryside. The tracks are

lined with sunflower fields. About an hour in we suffer some sort of mechanical failure. We watch as the train engineers walk past our window, looking quite routine. We pull our window down and something smells terribly burnt. Nevertheless, after 10 minutes or so we are running again, albeit at a noticeably slower clip. There are far worse places to suffer a breakdown than the Tuscan countryside.

It doesn't take long to size up Chiusi and decide we'd prefer an earlier train out of town. Peeking at the departure list, our original ticket is for 1:30pm, but there is an earlier train leaving at 10:57am. The only drawback is it's a local train, meaning it'll make more stops and be a bit slower. Even still, we should get there well before our original plan.

I speak to the station attendant and work out the change in broken Italian. He refunds us some money since we are taking a lower class train and bids us bon voyage. With 45 minutes now to kill, we wander out into town. It's a sleepy looking place with not much going on. It looks like there might be a more charming old town on the hill above us, but our legs decline to investigate. We find a park bench to rest on before heading back to the station. Jennie buys us some snacks, and we catch our connection to Rome.

Our train crosses into the region of Umbria. It features the same rolling hills and stony towns of Tuscany. I wonder how Tuscany gained the image and popularity it enjoys instead of Umbria?

Approaching the city, we come to a stop in a tunnel. We are stationary for 20 minutes or so, and the pressure has caused all the babies on the train to start crying. But even high pitched wails can't dampen our excitement as we pull into Roma Termini, the central station of the city of Rome.

10: ROME

We scurry out a side door of Termini, and Rome sprawls out before us and presses down upon us all at once. The city could easily be described as intimidating. And the young couple we had met on the La Spezia train platform were right. Italy's capital hits us with a hellish heat.

It's about a 2 mile walk from the station to the part of town our apartment is in. Within a couple of minutes we are drenched in sweat and miserable. We debate hailing a taxi, but decide we've made it this far on two feet, might as well finish the trip bipedal as well. We trudge on, block after block, occasionally stopping to admire a unique building, statue, or fountain.

We arrive early, and stop into Le Segrete, a small restaurant just around the corner from our meeting spot. Le Segrete has Wi-Fi, so I take the chance to message Federica, our host, to let her know we've arrived. After enjoying a couple plates of pasta Jennie and I reround the corner to our apartment building where Federica is waiting upstairs. She buzzes the door open and we enter. The stairs start immediately to our left, and we begin the spiral climb upwards. The room itself is 7 flights up, in the attic of the building, and our legs wobble and give by floor four.

Finally reaching the room, we greet Federica and get our keys. As soon as she leaves we pull the couch to make a bed and plop down under the AC unit to cool off. The room is small, but it has a sink and washing machine. Our clothes are starting to get smelly, so the washing machine is a very nice plus. The bathroom is laughably tiny, with no separation between the sink, toilet, and shower head. We laugh and joke about showering while we potty and brush our teeth at the same time.

We open the large window next to the bathroom to reveal a terrace looking out over the rooftops. In the distance we can see St. Peters Basilica and Square. We give the pope a wave, and retreat back to the AC for a while more. Jennie naps, and I dig into some maps to mark our must-see sights.

Venturing out into the dulled, but still absurd heat, we meander aimlessly through the streets. We buy some gelato and stumble in and out of a few impressive piazzas. Turning a corner, we come face to face with the Pantheon. It's scale is impossible to describe, and it might just be the coolest building I've ever been in. We walk past the groovy band playing in the square to a large crowd and pass through the large granite columns.

Inside, all eyes are immediately drawn up to the massive dome with it's famous "eye to the heavens" oculus cut out in the center. Almost two thousand years after it was built, the Pantheon's dome is still the world's largest unreinforced concrete dome. And it was built somewhere around 150 AD! I can't even begin to imagine the tools and techniques used to build the structure. It is one of the best-preserved of all Ancient Roman buildings, in large part because it has been in continuous use throughout its history, serving as a Christian sanctuary today.

The interior is densely packed with tourists, and signs

everywhere warn of pickpockets. My anxiety in large crowds, and general vigilance against pickpockets makes it hard to fully enjoy the scope of the building. We make our way around once and head back out through the columns. We listen to the band playing here for a few songs, and then follow signs pointing to the Piazza Navona.

Piazza Navona was used by the Romans as an open arena for games. In the 15th century, the city's market was moved here, and now it serves as a forum for artists and performers to sell their works. The inner square features a few fountains great for pictures and a light mist to cool off. We walk through the square, admiring artwork and watch a few of the street performances.

Back towards the apartment, we find a nice pizzeria a few doors down from our building. The owner greets us warmly and slices us generous portions of an herb covered marinara and cheesy pizza. We take seats in the back with a tall water and enjoy the meal. After a few minutes a most typical American tourist walks in with his money pouch dangling from his neck, fisherman hat, and white socks halfway up his calf and orders a few pizzas. The owner thanks him and tells him it'll be just a moment in perfectly understandable English. The American stays at the counter and proceeds to repeat his order. A series of miscommunications take place, and the insistent American guys demands to speak to the owner. "It is me!" The owner exclaims, and shoves the guy's pizzas in a box and shews him out the door. He rattles off some rapid Italian to his cook in the back before coming back to the counter, still clearly peeved. The pizza was very good, and we'd like to come back, so we make sure to thank him profusely before leaving. He appreciates this, and gives us a card and a coupon. We feel accepted into the community.

Back up the thousand stairs to our apartment, we crank the AC to high and read, write, and prepare for our first full day exploring Rome.

We wake up early in an attempt to beat the heat. We throw back a couple of espresso shots and make our way down into the streets. Today we are exploring Vatican City, and start heading west from apartment. Crossing to the other side of the Tiber River, we walk alongside it past the Castel Sant'Angelo. Built in the 2nd century, the towering cylindrical building has been used by popes as a fortress and castle, and is now a museum.

We cross to the Via della Conciliazione, the avenue which leads directly into St. Peter's Square. Finally, we get our first up close look at the Basilica ahead. But as soon as it comes into view, we begin to get harassed by peddling tour guides. These people are worse than used cars salesmen. Much worse. They follow us down the street shouting, and when we wave them off they call us ignorant. I wonder how many times they get punched by tourists with anger issues. I hope it's a lot.

The annoyances stop once we enter into St. Peter's Square. Apparently they are not allowed in to preserve the sanctity of the holy city. We bask in the views from the square and snap a few photos before entering the line for the Basilica. In line I'm peeved that the Vatican dress code listed on all the websites seems to be bogus. Tourists around us wear shorts and sleeveless shirts and aren't given a second look as we pass through security and the ticket counter. And here Jennie and I stand in pants and sleeves in the middle of a heatwave. Shenanigans.

We choose to start by taking an elevator up to the top of the basilica and walking around the inner base of the dome. Looking down at the floor gives you perspective on how huge St. Peter's really is. The people look like ants below. We walk around the side wall of the dome and out the other side, thinking that's it. But then we see an arrow pointing up saying "This Way." "To What? Heaven?" I ask Jennie.

Following the arrow we find ourselves spiraling upwards. The walls begin to close in on us and by the top we are hunched nearly all the way over. The heat rises with every step too, and there's no airflow to speak of. I can't help to think how a water vendor would absolutely make bank if one were to set up here. But it's all worth it when we reach the top. 360 degree panorama views of Vatican City and Rome spread out before us. We gaze out over the rooftops at the buildings, the parks, and can even in the distance see some of the Roman ruins we will visit tomorrow. We snap a few photos and try to catch our face in whatever breeze we can before descending again through the narrow stairs.

The stairway smells like a high school locker room. It's even covered in ugly green tile like many of the locker rooms back home. The stairs end on top of the basilica's roof. There are bathrooms and a water fountain. And perhaps the most typically Italian thing I've seen on the trip, there's also an espresso bar. On the roof of St. Peter's Basilica. Amazing.

We go in the espresso bar and get a large cold Sprite on ice. We decline to wait on the elevator, so we walk down even more spiral steps to reach St. Peter's floor. An attendant stops us before entering, making us finish our Sprite and throw it away. We enter and are immediately overwhelmed with the basilica's size and ornateness. It seems like you could hold 8 or 10 consecutive services in here and not interfere with another. The space is overrun with tours and selfie sticks. We snap some photos and admire the artwork for a while before the crowd pushes us out.

Outside the basilica, we buy tickets to enter the Sistine Chapel and Vatican Museums. We splurge and get the priority tickets, which essentially means a guy goes online and makes reservations for us like we should have done beforehand.

From St. Peter's Square we turn left and follow around the Vatican City border. Along the way we get shouted at from more tour guides. One gets far too close and is yelling nonsense in my ear so I brush him aside. He throws up his hands and starts screaming expletives. "F***ing entitled Americans." I'm not sure who would let this man guide them through the holy city.

Rounding the corner and approaching the entrance to the museum and Sistine Chapel we are immediately glad we sprung for priority tickets. The entrance line stretches for hundreds of yards. But we are able to walk directly to the front and walk right in. We try to use our tickets on the turnstiles inside before realizing we need to go to the reservation desk to exchange them for validated tickets. With the correct ticket in hand, we enter into the museum.

We head through the art exhibits first. Paintings and tapestries from all ages hang on the walls. Both Jennie and I like to look at the paintings, but I can't say either of us are too knowledgeable on the subject. Nevertheless, it's pretty cool to see the works of people like Raphael and Leonardo Da Vinci up close and personal.

The route to the Sistine Chapel presents us with two options, the short or long itinerary. We choose the long, and start weaving our way through courtyards filled with statues. We see thousands of statues and sculptures before entering a long corridor. The windows of the corridor are closed, and the air is stagnant. People crowd in and begin pushing their way along. To say we are crammed in like sardines would be an understatement. At any point in time in this corridor we are smushed against a minimum of 4 or 5 people. And the heat. Oh the heat is horrendous.

We push along the corridor for 15 or 20 minutes. The hall is beautiful I'm sure, but it is impossible to enjoy. I theorize that the Vatican wants us to feel the heat of hellfire before spilling mercifully into the climate controlled chapel.

I am about 30 seconds from passing out when we push through the final doors. Reaching the Sistine Chapel is refreshing, and it is definitely pretty. But again it's hard to fully enjoy as the guards continuously shush the crowd and force us to keep moving through. We step out of the line for a few moments to gaze at the ceiling, a masterpiece without precedent, and one that no doubt changed the course of Western art. Then a guard ushers us back into the line and out the door.

Outside, it's about 1pm and we've been going nonstop. We stop for lunch in a small dive bar interestingly named Knick Knack Yoda. They specialize in burgers, a break from our pasta and pizza binge. I get one with smoked ham, caramelized onions and barbeque sauce that is appropriately heavenly for its Vatican-side location. Jennie gets a traditional American cheeseburger for a little taste of home.

Energy slightly restored by lunch, we begin to trek back east towards our apartment. On the way, the city has set up an emergency tent to deal with dehydrated tourists and to hand out waters. We take a few and down them in no time. Retracing our route past Castel Sant'Angelo and across the Tiber, we cut down a few alleys and finally reach our apartment. Jennie and I both take cold showers before passing out for a much needed siesta.

Our legs feel like melted gelato. In the afternoon we slowly stroll through the streets of Rome, enjoying the architecture and weaving in and out of shops. We find our way to the Trevi Fountain, but are met with disappointment as it is drained and covered in scaffolding. We pretend the fountain maintains its romantic allure and share a few kisses, and head back the way we came.

We stop in for some pizza to-go and pick up some wine and snacks from a small shop. We set up our meal on our apartment's terrace and enjoy the evening air. It's still hot, and we're still sweating, but we don't mind anymore. We play cards looking out at St. Peter's and listen to the rhythms of the city.

The next morning we grab croissants and coffee at Giolitti's, a famous cafe and gelato shop. The day is to be filled with Roman ruins. We head southeast, well past the Pantheon. Soon, the Palazzo Venezia comes into sight. The large and looming palace lies just north of the Capitoline Hill, and our anticipation begins to grow.

Passing the Palazzo, we are immediately absorbed into history. To our right stretches the Roman Forum, surrounded by the ruins of important government and market buildings. It was for centuries the center of Roman public life: the site of triumphal processions and elections; the venue for public speeches, criminal trials, and gladiatorial matches; and the nucleus of commercial affairs. The teeming heart of ancient Rome, it has been called the most celebrated meeting place in the world, and in all history. We soak in the atmosphere.

We walk along the Forum, and approach the famous Colosseum. A line for entrance wraps around the outer edge of the structure, so we gaze at the exterior for a bit and make our way to Palatine Hill. Along the way we are heckled by tour guides. The line to enter the Palatine Hill is much shorter, and we are able to buy a double ticket for the Colosseum to use later.

Inside the gates for Palatine Hill, we stop in the shade for a moment to reapply sunscreen and catch our breath. We are now situated on the centermost and most ancient of the Seven Hills of Rome. From the emperor's residence, you can look down on the Roman Forum to the north, the Colosseum to the east, and Circus Maximus to the south. The ruins of the emperor's palace are massive. I can't begin to imagine how impressive this would have been in its time. There is no mistaking the power and grandiosity of the

Roman Empire.

As we look out over the remains of the Circus Maximus, a Brazilian guy from Sao Paulo approaches us. He's making a video for his girlfriend Julianna with different people in different languages saying "Julianna, you are beautiful." Jennie and I stand together and recite the phrase feeling silly, but glad we can help spur an international romance.

Walking back through some gardens we overlook the Forum on the other side of the hill. It is very much in ruins, with no rooftops standing and very few full height columns. Still, it's easy to imagine it filled with merchants and activity.

We march down off Palatine Hill, and circle around the Colosseum. The line has died down a bit, but we're off to find a lunch spot before entering. Following a street just to the east, there are plenty of tourist catering restaurants. We pick a table in one and order some pasta. Mine comes doused with cheese, but Jennie is awesome and trades me plates. In the end we end up sharing her far better plate of Penne in tomato and garlic sauce.

Next door we get some Nutella gelato. It's definitely closer to Nutella than gelato, as it tastes like it is straight out of the jar. This certainly isn't a bad thing, as we both could swim in a pool filled with the yummy hazelnut chocolate spread, but it isn't what we were expecting.

At the Colosseum there is barely a line at all. We walk right in and scan our tickets. Our excitement spills over with every new turn and view. We take our time reading the histories along the outer walkways. We are standing in the largest amphitheater ever built. It is widely considered one of the greatest works of architecture and engineering of all human history.

It is estimated the Colosseum could hold between 50,000 and 80,000 spectators, depending on the event and period of construction. Considering the stonework was pilfered for other construction projects, along with the structure surviving multiple earthquakes, it is in remarkable condition.

As we walk out into the arena we try to imagine the spectacle this place must have been nearly 2000 years ago. There is said to have been tarping strung and operated by sailors to provide shade and rain cover. And the wooden, sand covered flooring was cut with trap doors and elevator systems. The ingenuity and inventiveness it must have taken to develop and stage an event is staggering to think about.

We walk around the upper level a few times, taking pictures and eavesdropping on tour guides. We head downstairs and do much of the same on the lower level. We get into a conversation with a family from Iowa and take turns snapping photos for each other. I brag about my University of Tennessee Volunteers whooping up on their Hawkeyes in last year's college football bowl game.

With a last look and brief gladiator reenactment, we leave for the apartment. On our way back we stop often. Across the street from the Roman Forum we sit and admire the Forum of Augustus. This Forum was built to house a Temple of Mars, as well as serve as a house for legal proceedings, as the Roman Forum had become far too crowded. A few of the temple columns still stand and give an idea of just how large in scale the structure was.

Meandering along between the two forums, we approach a couple of guys with a table set up on the walkway. They shout and motion for us to come closer, unnecessary since we have to walk by them regardless. They start talking in hurried English about needing signatures for a petition of some kind. I wave my hand as I don't want to sign anything I don't understand. They start to get angry and tell us to sign once more, and I tell them no thanks we're not signing anything and walk on. They shout, telling everyone that can hear how worthless Americans are. Maybe it's just me, but that doesn't seem like the best way to attract tourists to your booth.

After a quick nap at the apartment, we find a grocery store for some food. We wash some greens and veggies and have a large salad with fresh lime and olive oil dressing. It's a wonderful meal and we enjoy it with some prosecco on our terrace. Jennie is beet red from the sun, and no amount of aloe can ease the burn. We call it a night early, around 9pm, drained from a long day in ancient Rome.

It's Saturday. Our last day to explore. We head out from our building with no agenda. We just want to walk and see what we're drawn into. We browse through the artisan shops a few blocks south of our apartment, and grab lunch at a small corner restaurant. We start to reflect on our trip and the fun we've had. We talk about our favorite spot and moment. Mine was drinking wine under the twinkling stars in Corniglia, overlooking the Mediterranean. Jennie murmurs and says I stole her favorite. We agree it's hard to pick anyways as the trip has been filled with amazing places, food, and views.

After lunch we begin gift shopping. I buy my mom a Pinocchio Christmas tree ornament, easy to find since Pinocchio is in every shop in all kinds of different forms. I didn't realize Pinocchio was still that popular. We look at hand crafted smoke pipes and old man driving caps and consider buying one for Matt, Jennie's brother. But she vetoes claiming Matt is already weird enough, he doesn't need an old man's cap to add the effect.

In the Piazza Navona we peruse the art and consider buying a couple pieces as our souvenir. We can't decide on one though, and begin to get frustrated with each other. The heat and exhaustion has worn us down, and down a side street we find a bench and hash out our feelings and vent a little. In the end, we decide to go back to Piazza Navona and buy a couple nice watercolors from a painter. They are great paintings, one of the Colosseum and the other of a sunflower field, but we both wish we had bought our souvenir from the lady on the Corniglia steps. To this day we haven't forgiven ourselves.

Out of the piazza, we stumble into a beautiful and ornate church. There are no other tourists, and the church is completely quiet. We sit and admire for a moment before the silence and lack of company makes the space eerie. We turn left out of the doors and follow the shade down whatever street it leads. The small alleys are lined with everything from cute artisan shops to expensive designer furniture stores. We enjoy window shopping for a couple of hours, taking our time to savor the environment.

Around 6pm we set out for the Spanish Steps. The Spanish Steps are just that, a large set of steps connecting two piazzas where locals and tourists alike gather in the evenings. The area around the Steps is filled with fashion stores and designer brands. There are many upscale restaurants as well, and we've picked one out for our last supper.

Il Gabriello is a highly reviewed family run restaurant tucked down in a cellar of an old building. The atmosphere is supposed to be incredibly romantic and charming. We find the small sign and open the wooden doors, making our way down the steep stone stairs into the lobby. The hostess, however, kills our plan immediately. She points to a sign on her desk. "Formal attire only, no shorts." I start to speak but she shakes her head and redirects us again to the sign. We retreat back up the staircase.

Around the corner we find a charming courtyard restaurant as plan B. Jennie enjoys an extra cheesy lasagna, and I have a peppery chicken and veggies plate. The meal is good, and it renews our spirit after my bare legs lead us to rejection.

There are so many wonderful and beautiful parts of Rome. The Spanish Steps are not included in those parts.

The area is overrun with people selling roses and selfie sticks. We stand with our backs against a wall taking in the scene and no less than 10 guys, hands full of roses, come up and try to force us to buy.

On our way back Jennie is about to pee on herself. There's nowhere to pop into with a public bathroom, so we have to power walk to the apartment and up the stairs. I jump a few stairs at a time to get to the attic door and have it open when she gets there. I've got a small bladder too so I know how the urgency feels.

Down the stairs once more, we walk to Giolitti's for our last serving of true gelato. We sit on a door stoop nearby and lament the end of our time here. At the same time, our legs are giving out, and we long for non-starchy food.

Jennie and I stuff our clothes in our bags and prepare everything for travel home. To end the night, we sit on the terrace taking in the city scape and say goodbye to the lights of the Vatican.

11: TO KNOXVILLE

Our alarm shrieks at 4:45am. We tidy up and shoot some espresso from our apartment's quick-brew machine and strap on our bags for the hike back to the train station. The air is cool, and the streets are nearly silent. We make it to Termini station in time for the 6:05am shuttle to Fiumicino airport.

We haven't had any food or water yet, and at this point I'm nearly dying of thirst. I begin to get dizzy and motion sick as the train beats its way down the tracks. As soon as the doors open I make for the small platform shop and buy a water. I'm rejuvenated nearly instantly.

We hop on a bus to Terminal 5, and make for the door. But we are stopped by two attendants and told we cannot enter until our departure is within two hours. Apparently a part of one of the main terminals had burned in a fire recently, and many of those airline desks had to be relocated out here to the distant Terminal 5. As such, the terminal is far too small for the situation.

A line forms for a while, as people wait to be admitted inside the doors for check-in. But eventually people begin to mob around the entrance and nobody has any clue what's going on. We sit on a bench on the outside wall and watch the chaos until it's nearly two hours before our flight bound for Montreal is to leave. We join the slow moving blob of people and eventually make it inside.

Checked in and through security, we are then shuttled across the tarmac back to T3, one of the main terminals. With an hour to kill, we eat and potty and wait at our gate. When our tickets are checked, we make our way down the tunnel just to be put in yet another shuttle bus. It takes across the tarmac once more and unloads us at the base of our plane. We wait for stairs to be attached and finally we load. In the air Jennie curls up and naps for most of the way. I try to do the same, but end up just watching her cute sleepy face for a good part of the flight.

We land in Montreal mid-afternoon. Storms are ravaging the area and flights have all been grounded. We prepare ourselves to be stuck here a while. A few naps and a terribly expensive Burger King meal kills some time, and sometime after midnight we are able to take-off bound for Washington DC.

We get stuck in DC's Dulles airport for what seems like days. We missed our connector by a long shot thanks to the Montreal lightning storms. It's around 2am when we arrive, and we get scheduled for an overbooked flight at 3pm. We find a dark corner and spread out on the empty benches. We try to sleep for a while and actually manage to squeeze in an hour or so of broken shut-eye. Eventually our dark and quiet corner is intruded upon by an obnoxious group who had been raising all kinds of annoying fuss at the customer service counter a few hours ago. They make their home too near to us, so we get up around 5am and wander the wings of the terminal like zombies.

We eat breakfast, and then lunch in the airport food court. When our 3pm arrives, we discover that I have a seat, but Jennie is going to get bumped. They offer us travel vouchers and we take them grudgingly. At this point, we just want to get home.

We are guaranteed spots on our next flight, but it doesn't leave until 10pm that night. We rub our eyes and retreat once more to a quiet corner of the terminal to wait. After our third food court meal, we find our gate and sit and stare at the clock.

Our plane touches down in Knoxville close to midnight. Our Italian honeymoon draws to a close with Jennie and I dragging ourselves down the hall and into the airport lobby. We poured everything we had physically and emotionally into the trip. And our memories of it are filled with love. And wine. And gelato.

ABOUT THE AUTHOR

Eric Wilhite is a husband, father, nerd, and author. He loves to travel and explore new cultures and ideas. He and his family live in the foothills of the Smoky Mountains. No matter where he travels to, he always seem to be drawn home to the Smokies.

Made in the USA
Monee, IL
14 December 2021